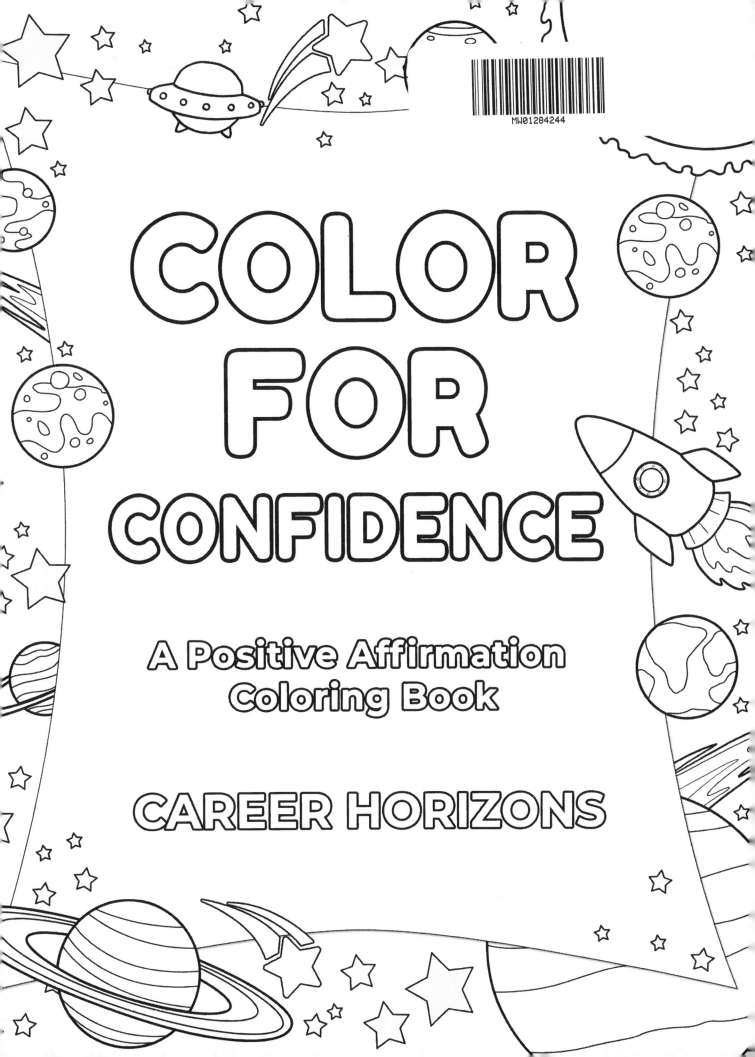

COLOR FOR CONFIDENCE

A Positive Affirmation Coloring Book

CAREER HORIZONS

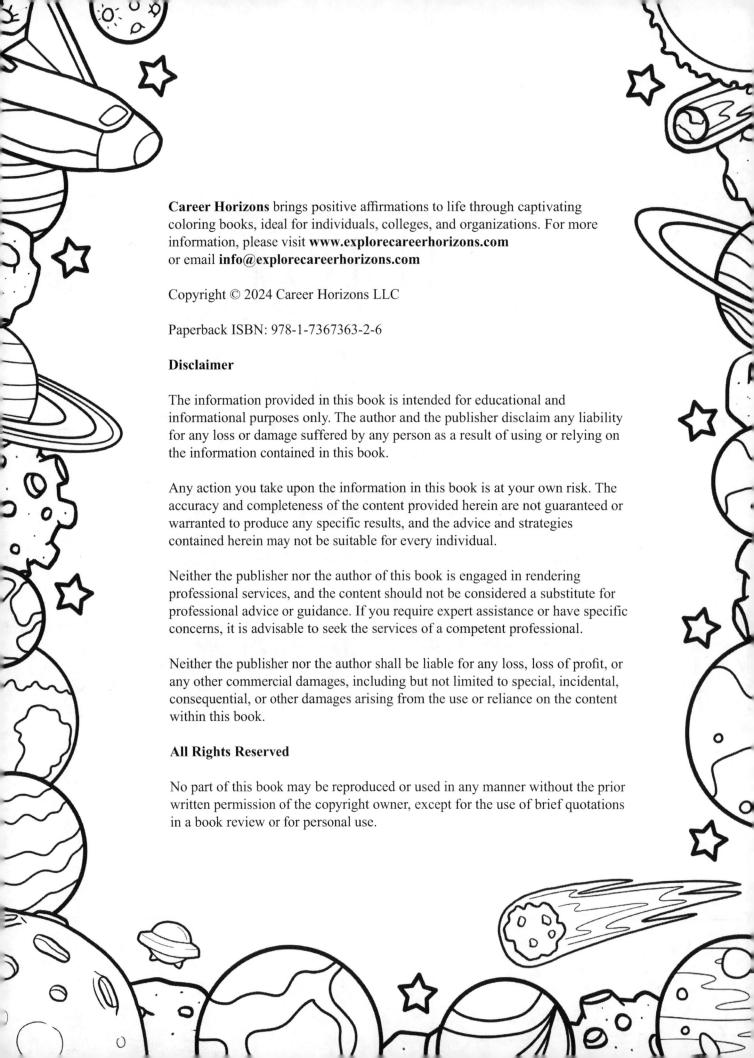

Career Horizons brings positive affirmations to life through captivating coloring books, ideal for individuals, colleges, and organizations. For more information, please visit **www.explorecareerhorizons.com** or email **info@explorecareerhorizons.com**

Paperback ISBN: 978-1-7367363-2-6

Disclaimer

The information provided in this book is intended for educational and informational purposes only. The author and the publisher disclaim any liability for any loss or damage suffered by any person as a result of using or relying on the information contained in this book.

Any action you take upon the information in this book is at your own risk. The accuracy and completeness of the content provided herein are not guaranteed or warranted to produce any specific results, and the advice and strategies contained herein may not be suitable for every individual.

Neither the publisher nor the author of this book is engaged in rendering professional services, and the content should not be considered a substitute for professional advice or guidance. If you require expert assistance or have specific concerns, it is advisable to seek the services of a competent professional.

Neither the publisher nor the author shall be liable for any loss, loss of profit, or any other commercial damages, including but not limited to special, incidental, consequential, or other damages arising from the use or reliance on the content within this book.

This book belongs to:

_____

Made in the USA
Columbia, SC
18 February 2024

31686248R00030